Musings

Jassimran Kaur

BookLeaf Publishing

India | USA | UK

Presentation by *BookLeaf Publishing*

Web: www.bookleafpub.com

E-mail: info@bookleafpub.com

ISBN: 9789358736151

First edition 2023

*For my grandmother,she isn't here today but
wherever she may be.*

Matah

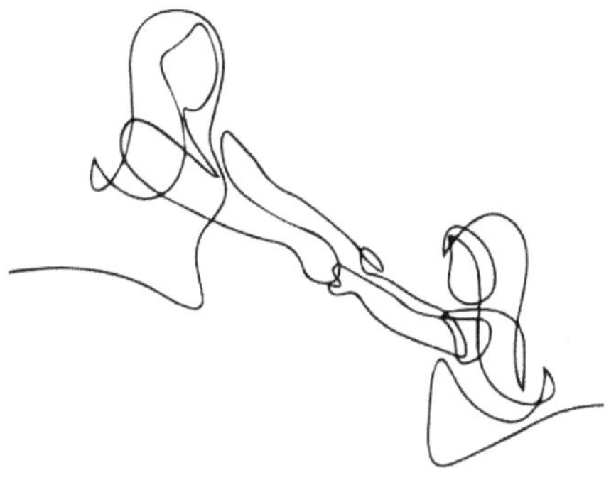

ਮਾਤਾ | Mother,
You were like my second
Only one who I'd let brush my hair when mum
couldn't,
Braiding it everyday before I set off to school,
Always making me late and missing the bus.
Chasing your son with that rolling pin,
Still covered in flour,
when he stole sneaky bites of my food.
The glare in your eyes when I spent too at the
market with friends and buying those old school
nestle chocolate bars.
Or when I skipped school to go climb trees in
the park,
only to come home with bloody knees and
scrapped elbows.

The tears glinting in your eyes when I spoke
about hiking Machu Picchu or climbing the
stairway to heaven.
You talked about my wedding,
How you'd interrogate my groom,
Readying your threats already.
You promised to stay,
but promises made to be broken.
I try to remember more but
now the pieces left don't really complete the
whole puzzle.
There are missing edges and frayed middles,
Leaving me to wonder now if I climb
the stairway now will you greet me at:
the end.
Maybe there won't be a staircase,
Or light at the end.
It could be another stage,
A second chance,
at a first life.
What a blessing that would be,
to know you again.
Another life.
Another reality.

It's always the silence

It's the silence that's painful.

When the noise outside isn't enough to drown
out your own thoughts,
the monster that follows you like a shadow,
gnawing in your veins.
Slithering around every thought,
desire, emotion.

Fear.

You become your own black hole, caving into
your very flesh and bone.
The blood rushing through your ears,
a sign of your own personal apocalypse.

Wrath

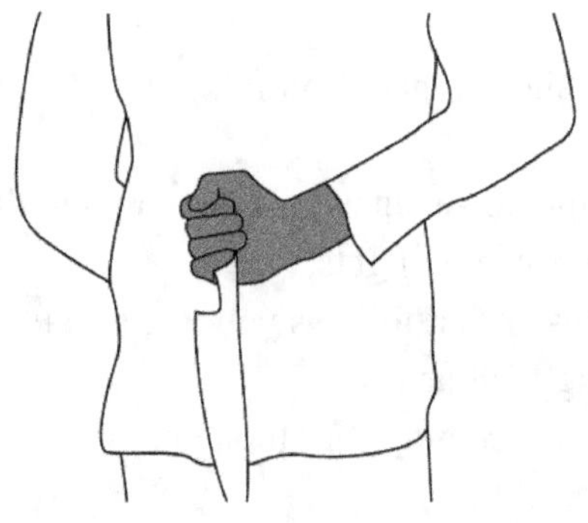

My anger isn't for me
It burns for my friends
My family,
a spark once lit
It Burns,
As I've grown,
So has my anger,
It burns less impulsive
In my veins I feel my blood rush hot
From my chest it branches into my arms
My legs and my fingertips
One touch and I may crackle
Crackle and became an inferno
Long have I craved to smother it
Cover it over,
let it fizzle,
cool under my skin.

Maybe it isn't simply anger,
But an ache,
A scab I keep peeling.
What a bad habit,
Hurt disguising as anger,
And me refusing to let it heal.

Random thoughts

Writing about fun seems fun
Until you try to find a way to describe it.
Other than fun I mean.
Then it's less fun.
Fun is the only way to say fun,
Because fun is fun.
Fun used to be swinging swings and sliding
slides.
The ice-cream cone waffery and chocolate filled.
Unless you like mint chocolate-chip,
That's a sin.
Now fun is the 7 shots at the bar,
The kiss goodbye on the front porch,
The morning after the night before.
I can tell you all the different ways to have fun
but without fun
It wouldn't be fun.
Like fun to me is climbing a tree
Or reading a book,

But to you it might be numbers of cars
Mustangs, Cameros or a little are micra
And karaokeing in tens of different bars.
Karaoke is never fun just a btw,
It's sad and awkward but absolutely oh soo fun.
Unless fun is your idea of hell.
Even Lucifer uses karaoke in his fun schemes
Fun is fun is fun
Nuf is nuf is nuf
Even Lucifer uses karaoke in his fun schemes
Unless fu is your idea of hell
It's sad and awkward but absolutely oh soo fun
Karaoke is never fun just a btw.
And karaokeing in the tens of bars.
Mustangs, Cameros or little grey micra
But to you it might be numbers of cars
Or reading a book,
Like fun to me is climbing a tree.
It wouldn't be fun.
I can tell you all the different ways to have fun
without fun
The after the night before
The kiss goodbye on the front porch,
Now fun is 7 shots at the bar
That's a sin.
Unless you like mint chocolate-chip
The ice cream cone wafers and chocolate filled.
Fun used to be swinging swings and sliding
slides

Because fun is fun,
Fun is the only way to say fun
Then it's less fun.
Other than fun I mean,
Until you find a way to describe it,
Writing about fun is fun.

Pain

How can you know anything about pain
You lose your life on a regular

There's no fear in you,
A little bit of blood and you'll regain your
strength

You'll wake with your belly full,
No worries on your mind

I'm still here,
exactly where I was last night.
Still watching her body,
Waiting, hoping, praying for her to wake,
She won't.
I know that but can't force my brain to believe
it,
She's human.

You pretend for a living,
Faking or as you call it
Acting.
The blood surrounding you isn't yours,
It isn't anyone's, it's nothing but coloured
cornstarch.

Another fake.

It wasn't like that for her,
the blood wasn't visible,
But the bags under her eyes were
Her body was still,
Vacant.
And she was lost.

Nana won't wake,
She isn't like you.
She's human.

Gibberish

I talk and talk and talk,
You hear me,
Your eyes give tell me that.
Yet you haven't listened,
Have you?
Maybe I sound blurred to you,
As if I'm underwater,
Maybe I am,
These breaths are shallow,
These hands shaky.
But I can't tell where the line is drawn,
Whether it's anger or hurt in my bones.
Time passes,
A month, a day or a year,
 I'm still talking,
Hoping this will be the time you listen.
Do you?

Roots

Maybe I'm the branch,
The diseased one in my family tree. Rotting.
Infecting. Decaying.

A Thursday Anecdote

I saw a blind man today, he was navigating
London tubes. Now if you aren't aware london's
underground system is one of the most
confusing and I struggle even with many years
of experience.

Anyway, it made me wonder, life is similar.

Many of us can see but still choose to stumble
through every little hurdle in our way, the
smallest inconvenience throwing us off track and
yet here was this man freely walking into the
largely unknown; freely without fear.

Humans

What if we aren't the gift?
What if babies aren't the blessing,
Instead humans a virus in disguise.
Self proclaimed knights; are we though,
We created wars and violence,
We cheat, we lie
Blaming it all on our 'humanity'
To the earth we are not its protectors,
Nor its savours,
but the curse.

Light and dark

I'm not used to early mornings, being awake
before the skies themselves.

Watching the dark crack into dawn, black
turning into a warming orange.Or a steely grey if
you're in England like me.

There is light now though, even through the
grey, it illuminates the morning. For some
reason it reminds me of us, the way we all hide.
Trying to keep strictly to the dark or the light,
never truly acknowledging both. Always taught
that darkness equals evil. And light means good.

That's what all the films and fairytales suggest:
you are either a villain or a hero. Never both.

A turning point

Beauty comes within a breath. The breath of a sunset, as the sky shifts. Rose hues fade into a ray of peaches then burn into amber. Blink. It's transformed into a storm grey, scattered clouds forming an archway for first darkness. It never disappears, just conceals itself until the next day. Beauty is found by those who aren't afraid to search the darkness.

Orphic

Like a sea parting for Moses, the clouds separate creating an archway for Apollo himself. It's a breathtaking site, one that causes my heart to skip. Not in nerve or fright, but in pure awe.

For that moment I have left my body, witnessing the vastness of earth.

It's a moment of marvel to experience such a sensation.

A mortal conundrum

Through the past ages and the future ones, it would always be like this.

For if life and death can never coexist, how could you and I.

Laconic

I crave to know the meaning of life yet desire nothing more than to understand my part in yours.

A hidden dream

I read poetry for company,
To sit with my joys, sorrows
my hopes and my regrets.

And write in hopes
that my words too,
will matter to someone,
somewhere,
Somehow.

Reminisce

There's a strange peace
I stare and I see
Blurs of silouettes,
Memories;
Wishing on dandelions,
Watching them dance in the breeze,
The summer sun on my skin,
Cosy,
Crunching autumn leaves in the park,
Rolling the next piece of the snowman,
it isn't yet whole (like me)
But it will be (like me)
I stare at mirror,
Who is it that stares back?
Is it me or a memory.

Self reflection

'To be or not to be' as Shakespeare said.

As if it's a simple choice as if there is a clear
line between the two worlds.

As if you don't always drift between the waves,
crashing for one shore to the other.

Being, not being;
Both the light and the dark of your deepest self.

Opia

There was a pause, a sudden intake of breath, a
moment of silence when our eyes met.
Opia.

It wasn't that the world stood still but that our
souls finally sighed,
and whispered,
home.

Paradise

Home is me.
This body isn't just a host but
A cage trapping my data.
Once Eden was paradise
Now a simple apple takes over so many souls.
Batteries of phones die only to kill us over and
over.
The garden may be gone but in its place
Reigns this new realm of apples and
blackberry's
Of artificial intelligence instead of faith.
Paradise is not the same paradise as it was
before Christ
There aren't the same demons with beady blood
eyes and big claws
Now demons are hands on keyboards,
Faceless identities.
Masks upon masks,

Hiding in their shadows.
In the age of wireless
We still crave old connection
A heart that beats without a WiFi password.
Home is me,
the same me who spent a youth climbing guava
trees.

Musings

I'm not really sure what love is,
I don't mean the familial love
or the warmth you feel for dear friends.
I mean the love of a whispered promise,
A lingering kiss,
Or a gentle touch ,
The comfort of arms around you,
An assurance of them,
Almost an extension of your soul.

Softly spoken pacts,
promises,
Of knowing every marking,
Ever scar of each other,
Physical or not,
Understanding one another,
Every desire,
Every dream.
I hope for that,
My love, the other piece of my soul.

What is poetry?

What is poetry?
I used to wonder if it was Shakespeare or Poe
who had it figured out,
but now I ask whether it's Atticus or Halsey.
Maybe poetry is like time,
Without solid expectation or realisation.
It ebbs and flows, changing as do hands on a
clock; as seasons do.

Maybe poetry is simply a jumble of words,
strung together from our individual experiences,
our memories.
No longer is it rhyme or rhythm,
But a confession of my mistakes, my
melancholy, my musings.